MW01174497

I thought elvis was italian

I thought elvis was italian
Domenico Capilongo

WOLSAK
& WYNN

© Domenico Capilongo, 2008

No part of this publication may be reproduced, stored in a retrieval system or transmitted, in any form or by any means, without the prior written consent of the publisher or a license from The Canadian Copyright Licensing Agency (Access Copyright). For an Access Copyright license, visit www. accesscopyright.ca or call toll free to 1-800-893-5777.

Cover art: Lise Fournier
Author Photo: Lynda Anthony
Cover design: Rachel Rosen
Typeset in Adobe Garamond, printed in Canada by The Coach House Printing Company, Toronto, Ontario

The publishers gratefully acknowledge the support of The Canada Council for the Arts, the Ontario Arts Council and The Department of Canadian Heritage for their financial assistance.

Wolsak and Wynn Publishers Ltd
69 Hughson Street North, Ste. 102
Hamilton, ON
Canada L8R 1G5

Library and Archives Canada Cataloguing in Publication

Capilongo, Domenico, 1972-
    I thought elvis was italian / Domenico Capilongo.

Poems.
ISBN 978-1-894987-22-6

    1. Italian Canadians--Poetry. 2. Children of immigrants--Poetry. I. Title.

PS8605.A64I28 2008   C811'.6   C2008-901377-8

Before Elvis there was nothing.
–John Lennon

for Lynda

Contents

1

I thought elvis was italian   13
riunione   15
mortadella   16
toronto   18
appendix   20
grandfather   21
kneeling beside her   22
subtitles   23
ferrovia   24
the three tenors   25
the bricklayer   26
roma   28
this strange place   29
solo in giappone   31
alone in japan   32
if I could talk to him   33

2

shera-lee   37
corner church   38
spazio   39
january   40
I knew you when you loved me   41
chan chan   42
meadow trail   44
I have known you   45
out the window   46
green corners   47
take a deep breath   48

3

lesson   50
sensei   51
karate   53
karate legends   54
push past midnight   55
daruma   56
narrow road   57
otosan   58
under moon   63
morning   65
fuji   66
kinkakuji, the temple of the golden pavilion   68
yokohama dentures   70
karma police   71
hong kong, china   72
nha trang, vietnam   73

4

a clever title that hints at the poem's theme   77
aaron   78
audrey   79
van   80
wrong   81
you   83
cole's notes   84
variations   87
somewhere we have never travelled   88

1

Silence was never written down
–Italian proverb

I thought elvis was italian

pictures of my father slick-haired & sideburned
my uncles had all his albums
older cousins played the hawaii concert
whenever I was over
thought he had to change his name
like dean martin did

the leather
the rings & gold chains
the way he moved his hips
his lips
the leather
the sicilian black of his hair
the way he borrowed the tune of "o sole mio"
for his song "it's now or never"
his best friend named esposito
the leather
his fixation with cars
the way he looked at women
the way he put on weight
how close he was to his mother
the leather
the black velvet posters in everyone's basement
movies dubbed in italian
he was played at weddings after tarantellas
the leather
the rings
gold chains

if he's still alive he's in his 70s
eyeing his blood pressure
sitting in the courtyard of his villa
in some tiny southern italian village
deserted by emigration
a new graceland

talking sideways since the stroke
he sometimes plays the mandolin
sings in an ancient dialect
known only to farmers
he smiles at chickens
who peck at his feet
cats dance in the shade
his eyes moving slowly
under a mediterranean sun

riunione

my father in the early seventies
off the plane or was it a boat?
in halifax or montreal
then on the train for toronto
eating a packed lunch
the sound of english
strange union of letters on every sign
the sudden silence
first few weeks of acclimatization
reunion with grandparents & lost brothers

the small town confidence slipping slowly from his stride
with every stare at every bustop
only the suck from his cigarette
tilt of his hips
elvis presley, marcello mastroianni
will save him
his hands in their late teens begin to harden
look strange to him in this new country
the cold gripping of the bones

it's in the restaurants on danforth avenue or coxwell
where he's left to point out his orders like a mute
the cook gets to know his face
they never speak
& it's on the bus where he sees her again
not since childhood
since her older sister married his uncle in sicily
& there she was on the bus
they met
maybe were meant to meet
held onto each other in a common language
familiar movement of the eyes
skin
colour of the hair
the taste of a country left behind

mortadella

we had to drive two hours
all the way to regina
for coldcuts & panini

frustrated my father
bought wine grapes
borrowed a turtle pool
the one with the slide

we called neighbours & friends
washed our feet
poured in the fruit
dancing grapes
between our toes

the only italians in swift current
saskatchewan

neighbours amazed at our garden
my mother's angelic pasta
father's backyard buildings
whispered the word
mafia
behind closed curtains

kids at school
surprised at my talking hands
never traded lunches
with the kid from the country
shaped like a boot

back in toronto
mother speaking italian on the phone
watches telelatino
aunts & uncles
whom I barely know
ask me when I'm getting married
stare at my hair & ripped jeans

mortadella is just round the corner here
everyone is drunk on caffe latte

toronto

the feeling of my father's hand
pulling me up concrete steps
opening the door
we step out
on top of the world

in my memory
we had walked the whole way up
I forgot the elevator
the zipping ride

it was just me and papa
he was taller than any building
to me he had built everything

      he was there trading with the huron
      at their meeting place
      helped etienne brulé steer into shore
      my father nicknamed the city muddy york
      he fought the flames of 1904
      swept the streets of ashes
      he bought and sold apples in kensington
      prayed for victory in europe
      he ran hooch hidden in his jacket for al capone
      he mixed it up at the riots in christie pitts
      my dad brought war vets home
      he paved the streets of little italy
      my father captained the first subway
      he drove the zamboni at the gardens in '67

he lifts me up
I can feel the wind
swirl around in my left ear
I grab tightly around his neck
his moustache brushing my cheek
"look, maybe you can see our house from here"
I sneak a peek
see his giant finger
as big as buildings
pointing over this city

appendix

I died at seven
my stomach bursting
a bomb
the slow splitting
of internal atoms

the doctor says
it's just indigestion
give him some ginger ale

the night I died
my body folded
like a briefcase
of plutonium

my father carried me into the e.r.
as if we were models for
michelangelo's pieta

he tells the nurse my name
the same as his dead father's
it hangs in the air
until I wake up
and become a string of vowels

grandfather

they named me after him
when I was a boy he died
there are pictures of me in
blue-jeaned bell-bottoms holding his hand
chasing pigeons in an italian town square

when I was two years old
we spent a lot of time together
he whispered secrets in my ear
carried me on his shoulders
I don't remember

I look at his picture & his eyes move
his voice his breath against my ear
sometimes I dream of him
I never understand what he's saying

kneeling beside her

sleeping on the west coast. north vancouver. young boy. a dream.
back in the toronto basement of my father's aunt's house. 1st
floor. 2nd floor. dimly-lit staircase leading up to catacombs of
polished wooden tables. plastic-covered chesterfields. in the
basement a small kitchen. dining room table. great uncle smelling
of his leather shoe store. their bedroom a shrine of ceramic
madonnas. toddler swings & playpens for nieces, nephews &
grandsons. she sat on the old green couch beside the furnace. *la
nonna*. family grandmother. an heirloom of a village left behind.
she comes to me in flashes of photographs. a dream. she's lying
down. I'm kneeling beside her pumping her hand like petting
a kitten. our eyes lock. her mouth pedaling last words that I
can't make out. the damp basement surrounds us. wake up the
morning after. confused & sweaty. my mother tells me last night a
phone call.

subtitles

watches t.v. in english
weaves her own narrative
tells us what's really happening
spits her opinion out loud

sees things
shadows in her room
calling out to her husband
the one I'm named after
calls out to him
till he disappears
till it's quiet again

she tells us the dead will walk again
we have to keep our houses clean
she laughs like nostradamus
our *nonna*

caught talking to herself
has spread rumours like
sicilian bush fires

sitting at the corner of tables
eternal matriarch
she follows our english
like the hands of a roman calligrapher
hieroglyphs of the body
you can hear the words forming
in the edges of her eyes

ferrovia

knees clenched
holding on to the edges of her coat
as if this will save her

on the subway
under this city
this language
heavy on her like tons of earth

she pulls out a handful of pennies
each time the subway stops
she puts a penny back into her purse

people stare
she smiles
explains in italian
as if they understand

last penny
empty palm
she exits

the three tenors

tuxedoed valet boys
bursting at the seams
the tall slick-haired placido trying his hardest to upstage
the short carreras
the one my father thinks really captures the neopolitan dialect
even though he's spanish
then there's pavarotti
the bearded fat one
his thick eyebrows become outstretched hands
he feels every note like he's about to cry
like he's been caught in bed with a woman half his age

    enter bugs bunny
    the room falls silent
    his ears pushed back
    leopold leopold leopold
    he steps up to conduct
    lifts his hand high
    all three singers
    struggle to hold the note
    he drops it down and they sweat
    to follow him

my father in his basement
closing his eyes is back in italy
running through the streets
of his small hometown near naples
as a boy I listened
wishing I could travel on his eyelids
through narrow streets
the italian sun rounds the corner
hitting us

o sole
o sole mio

the bricklayer
after Michael Ondaatje

if I were a bricklayer
I'd smoothen the sheets of your bed
leave the smell of sweat & concrete
on your pillow

my rough hands
your breasts, shoulders, inner thighs
would burn, red
you could never go to super markets
not like other women
"it's the way she walks,"
they'd say

dry skin of your elbow
bags under brown eyes
tired hands
that massage my sore back
make my food
you'll age ten years
you'll be known as
the bricklayer's wife

before marriage
I could never
whistle from work sites
or touch you
– your sicilian mother, carpenter brothers
I showered
dressed my hands in white gloves, a tie
soaked my wrists in aftershave

I touched you once on st. clair
in the crowded street
you wore a red sweater
no one saw
I left your skin scarless
you stopped mid-step & said

        hey, this is how you touch other women
the butcher's wife, the mechanic's daughter
& you searched your skin

        what's the use
marrying the pizzamaker, or the barber
 with their smooth hands
it's like not making love at all

you pulled
my hand to your breasts
& said I'll make you lunches
of mortadella & provolone
touch me
I'm the bricklayer's wife

roma

this city sits on your shoulder
soaks into your skin
you taste different
on this *penisola*

an "o" on the end of every kiss
beside the buzz of speeding *vespe*
cappuccino foam licked air

the first time we saw
emanuele's monument
the gasp of breath
the curve of your leg
lower back
you eclipsed
everything

all roads
lead to you

roma falls on us
by accident
like lost tourists
searching for god
at every turn
along every *via*

I want to jump
into this *fontana*
between blades of sunlight
let this place
wash us like a
tempesta

this strange place

in sicily after the war. after the songs of mussolini. his capture
and death at the hands of his own men. after the allies rolled
into villages. in the predawn men meet in piazza town squares
and wait for local farmers to choose extra hands. like school boys
waiting to get picked on the favoured team. how many times
passed over before the rumours of *l'america* sound appealing? the
streets are paved in gold. there is work for everyone. returning
women gloating in markets telling stories of men sending money
home. how long before it's your turn? your wife's last kiss. the
picture of your infant son imprinted on the palm of your hand.
you board a ship. one suitcase. one pair of shoes. your surprise at
finding out you are seasick.

met by trees. the first signs of this country. the smell of a strange
place. the sound of a language unknown. following a line of short
men. the barren landscape of lost dreams and he suddenly realizes
that this is a place he has not even seen in nightmares. his knees
weak and eyes fearful. here he is a boy. a cramped house. the
woman with a deep voice shows him his room. enough for the
shape of one mattress. for one dog. he meets the man who will
use this bed during the day while he works.

first snowfall a dream. the beautiful soft floating sky. like slow
falling cheese. he misses his wife. the cold wraps around his bones
like leather. like the grip of death. made to dig the street for
sewer pipe while people in fancy cars drive by staring. *we are the
others here, our language, our skin unpleasant, the way we move our
hands between words, the way we stand and talk on street corners,
against the law here.* WOP. this word. the first time hits him like
a wet slap to the face. he writes to his wife and tells her about the
beautiful trees the falling flakes of white powder. he tells her not
to come. she doesn't listen.

enough to buy a house. a car. plant a garden. your wife takes a job sewing dresses. your son grows up with two tongues. two brains. he wears this new country, strange language, like a jacket. everything is all right. everything is in its place. in the darkness of your basement near the bottom of a glass of wine you are happy to have made things better.

solo in giappone

quando il sole muore
e la notte mi copre come il raffreddore
il telefono muto e silenzioso
i rumori della strada entrano senza permesso
il ballo del vento
l'autostrada che non dorme mai

quando chiudo gli occhi e non mi viene sonno
il frigo mi parla con i suoi brividi
la voce della mamma
mi chiama per mangiare
la nonna mi fa ricordare di lavarmi le mani
frattelli che mi prendono in giro
e papa`, seduto in canottiera, mi domanda come sto

si sente l'odore della pasta
e la musica della forchetta
che canta contro il piatto

alone in japan

when the sun dies
and the night covers me like a cold
the telephone mute and silent
the noise of the street enters without permission
the dance of the wind
the highway that never sleeps

when I close my eyes and sleep doesn't come
the fridge talks to me with its shivers
the voice of my mother
calls me to eat
my grandmother reminds me to wash my hands
my brothers poke fun at me
and dad, sitting in his undershirt, asks me how I am

I can smell the pasta
the music of the fork
that sings against the plate

if i could talk to him

i would tell him everything is all right
hiding in the corner of his bedroom
curled up like a fetus
angry voices seeping through in waves
under the door
vibrating between cracks in the wall
broken dishes
he doesn't really know what's happening

i would tell him everything is fine
hold his tiny hand
he tries to escape
by crossing his eyes
into the fabric of his blanket
into the floating dust captured
in slow motion
in beams of light shafting through the window
he cups his hands over his ears
shutting out the sounds echoing
in operatic crescendos

when it stops
it's like smoke settling
leaving him helpless to open the door
into the silent hallway

if i could talk to him
hold him
tell him everything will be better
not to be afraid of this moment

now at the bank
a busy corner of a shopping mall
or in the silence of a lover
he can sense tension rising
like a subtle change in the wind
he wants to run
hide his head between books

i would tell him he is not responsible
doesn't have to fix everything
there's no one here
who can hurt him
now

2

The heart has its reasons of which reason knows nothing.
-Blaise Pascal

shera-lee

first girl I kissed
not an elementary school brush of the lips
a kiss where you feel
the heart in the throat

on the canadian prarie
at the edge of the lake
walked her to her cottage
one hand on her fence
leaned forward
didn't know whether I should close my eyes

certain smell in the prairies
dryness that sticks to the nostrils
grasshoppers jumping with every step
bursting against the front of our speeding car

lips touched
I pushed forward
teeth hit
moon licked lake
the porch light a glowing satellite
she slipped her tongue into my mouth

corner church

deserted parking lot
some corner church
squirming into the backseat

i take your hand
we waltz out of our clothes like
abandoned snakeskin

opening the windows
lets our breath crawl
through tree branches

spazio

movement of stars
slipping from p.m. to a.m.
through time zones
dreams forgotten
frantic pupils
super nova
out of body
language
I dream of you
milky
cosmic kisses
satellite stepping stones
borrowed time
reach across the galaxy
of this bed
planet of your body
moon
I orbit you

january

windows keep the city outside. like this. the day creeps up on us
into the corners of the room. into the corners of our eyes. you're
warm. like this. as if the moon spent the whole night soaking into
you. I'm jealous. like this. here beside you floating above me. I
want to paint the room chagall blue. like this. there's a white goat
beside the bed. yellow clowns across the ceiling. like this. I dream
of you. your body. the way it fits mine. like this. the taste of you
in the memory of my mouth. restless I touch you. like this.

I knew you when you loved me

when your voice was the familiar sound of rain against the porch. the day & everything. the moon. the sun. & I knew you when you listened instead of staring at my mouth. when the movement of clouds held meaning. when your smile, a simple whisper of lips on teeth. the curling edges of your eyes. I knew you when we could touch in public, lace our fingers through passing cars & stop oncoming traffic. I knew you when every changing moment was filled with the curls of your hair. the scent of you hovering round my head. the edges of fingertips. I wore you then. a favourite t-shirt.

chan chan

walks from *altocedro* to *marcané*
from *cueto* to *mayarí*

his cigar
guides him
a glowing beacon

his hat
brown from the dust
of sugar cane fields
you can see the salsa tempo
in his step
under this cuban moon
he sings of her

> *el cariño que te tengo*
> *no te lo peudo negar*

the smell of her neck
juanica silhouetted
in his mind
on the beach
the line of her body
calls him
through her dress

> *se me sale la bibita*
> *yo no lo puedo evitar*

chan chan will walk
all night
he will walk
the lip of the moon
the edge of the earth
to see her

when I see her
I will hold her
I will put my lips
on her shoulder
and I will sing

de altocedro voy para marcané
llego a cueto, voy para mayarí

meadow trail

feels like summer's taking its last gasp of air with the sun. clouds
hang out in the distance waiting. the day can't decide what
season to be. we walk into this meadow. hands joined. the feel
of your skin changing temperature against the wind that bites
you in kisses. your pale green wool knit sweater fits the mood as
the dying field engulfs us in waves of thistle & shrubs that are
so worn they've lost their name. every so often there's a sprinkle
of summer's last heartbeat in purple firefly flowers peaking out
in patches as if to remind us that they will return in tranquil
whispers.

the trail dips down to the edge of a lagoon where the air has
become crisp & face numbing. as we round the water the wind
picks up. sky darkening. we laugh at the thought of our umbrella
sitting lonely in the back seat of the car. hardly notice the sky
beginning to fall in specks of white hail drops stuck into your
hair, my beard, feels like we are joined in a connect-the-dots
puzzle.

in the distance the remains of a stone cabin where I pull you close
to me together. the day stops spinning. I taste you as the season
falls apart.

I have known you

before our first kiss
first touch
before this place we call now
in mountains
in the origins of time
in himalayas
where gods are born
I saw you there walking
through waterfalls a dream

out the window

about to rain
sky holding off
bite of the lower lip
like a lover about to come
you can smell it
cool slow breeze
teasing memory of raindrops
skin goose bumped anticipation
heart of sky beating
just that much faster
fist full of hair
back of the head
tree branches swaying
leaves high speed metronomes
breath
slow motion tilt of the chin
sweat building in the curve of the back
sky a grey bed sheet
pressure of clouds pushing together
an eruption of first raindrops

green corners

(end moon moving this edge of night slips into sounds of traffic
river bed motions of subway tracks trembling under nightmares
of cockroaches radio dramas in british english teeter tottering
over shadows in green corners knowing when to retire this
endless competition of sleepless poses and heart beat rhythms
of insomniac television stations sending radioactive waves into
the skull of the next day makes me wait in anticipation for the
changing face of the moon

take a deep breath

take a deep breath. shadows stuck against the wall. reach out for
the sky. sometimes it feels like floating. sometimes you can't pick
your feet up off the floor. take a deep breath. the sound into small
specks of light. into time. see how the earth is turning. step into
the footsteps of a friend. take a deep breath. move slowly. the sun
crawling across a sheet of blue. make a long distance call. listen to
the fridge. it speaks into the corners of rooms in ancient tongues.
take a deep breath. hang out laundry when it's windy. sometimes
it's important to sleep with your socks on. spread your arms across
the floor. your heart beating like the tremble of an egg yolk. take a
deep breath. sip tea. the steam finding places we have never been.
sometimes if you walk slowly you can see the rays of the sun. take
a deep breath. feel the seconds suck between your teeth. time to
fish the moments out from the hollow of the ear. stretch your
fingers over someone's face. let them speak into your palm. listen.
take a deep breath. slow. long. breath.

3

I don't know karate, but I do know ka-razy.
–James Brown

lesson

I can teach you to punch
to stand as though you are sitting on a horse
to kick in four directions
shout from the pit of your belly
crouch like a cat about to pounce

I can teach you to block
to move like bamboo swaying in the wind
to kick in midair
fight on one leg like a crane
split a board with the edge of your hand

it's when you ask me
what to do in that moment
the schoolyard spinning
with laughter
as you pick yourself up off the ground
tears bursting
your chest heaving
hands already in fists

when you ask me
which kick?
what stance?
how to strike back

close your eyes
try to listen
to the calmness of clouds
pull the air in slowly

jump and kick
the humiliation from your shoulders
land and ground your stance firmly
into all the greatness that you know you are
move away as smoothly as a light breeze

sensei

> There was always the 'untaught hold'
> by which the master defeated
> the pupil who challenged him.
> —Michael Ondaatje

we face each other
I know I could smash
his knee
or maybe
with a flurry of punches
crack his ribs
his jaw

     almost thirty years my senior
     I have watched his body age
     while my body hardened
     he taught me how to move
     how to punch
     how to use my fist
     my feet

I could sweep
his front foot
pull him to the ground
and finish him

     I walked into the *dojo*
     barely a teen
     the sound of his voice
     never giving up on me

I move to the side
should I jump?
kick him in the chest
in the head?

sen to go before
sei life

I attack with my front hand
in the moment of hesitation
my mind full of scenarios
he slides into my punch
his body moving in slow motion
I feel the palm of his hand
strike softly the tip of my chin

karate

the white of the suit
the black of the belt
the chop suey movies dubbed in english
you have insulted my family
and the shaolin temple
prepare to die
the mister miyagi
wax-on-wax-off archetype
the *how many boards can you break?* party question
or *are your hands registered with the police?*
followed nervously by
have you ever had to use it?

there is a moment in the *dojo*
everyone in orderly lines
the sound of *sensei's* voice echoes
us moving at the same time
the feeling of my arm slicing the day
my body relaxes
muscles just tense enough to move bone
bare feet barely lifting
the width of thin rice paper
my mind
clean of thought

the moment of wind between bamboo
water trickling over river rock
the smooth light of the sun edging a whiff of cloud
a moment where
I don't need to know how fast I could take a life
there is peace and harmony
in this one punch

karate legends

secrets whispered
from master to student
father to son
in *dojo* training hall corners
of superhuman techniques

it has been said that ancient masters
in mid-battle could
through the use of trained abdomen muscles
pull their testicles up into their body
in order to protect themselves
from lower attacks

the deep breathing
contracting and relaxing of the stomach
the layers of muscle fibre
the last sucking breath in the back of the throat
pigeon-toed feet at the final moment
the dull sound of body entering body

my three-year-old nephew
walks towards me through the kitchen
swings his arm
like a world class cricket player
hits me full on in the groin
the blood rushing up to my ears

death. first his father. then his mother. can't be late. trains rolling
in on second hands. to believe. sun setting. settling in the clouds
an egg yoke. trees leafless reaching up for nothing. so far. they
sell everything. baked potatoes from half-bed trucks. the neckties
slipping. time to down another *asahi* beer before the next train.
phone rings. alarm clock. the dial tone. the ceiling leaking for
hours. four hours sleep. the school bell holds the note one second
too long. call a paramedic. desks pushed together for lunchtime.
he'll be home for one month. black tie and armband. nothing
stays the same so far. sons and daughters sleep hours ahead.
numb. here language is a veil. fragile. delicate. we must hide our
faces. the stores are closing with a smile and a bow. the rain falling
right on schedule. to believe. his world now stands on its head.
there's no place like home. like home. no place to hang my hat.
one day or two it will all be clear. a pair of glasses for my fiftieth.
maybe a telescope. phone our parents to hear them breathe. he
walks through empty rooms checking cupboards for shadows.
silhouettes of a past life. there's no time for slow steps. someone's
always waiting.

daruma

left with the cherry-blossomed afternoon
the day stuck between seasons
the fox a messenger for the gods
I wait for nothing to happen
so I can get on with it
it's the *jizo* buddhist statues at intersections that scare me
the smiling red-bibbed *bosatsu* know too much
have saved the souls of dead children
far too often
if they could only speak the words of 1000 years
like the spirit of the crane
to live forever
a dream in the white-powdered floating world
I want to ride a turtle
down to the dragon palace
where nothing matters
and times passes like bubbles of oxygen
the *daruma* doll
red and round
looks at me laughing
his eyes white and empty

narrow road

moving across this country
the sound of *shinkansen* bullet trains
echo like a string of *shamisen* guitars
I can't help but think of basho
walking
his haiku coming to him
as if carved
on the barks of trees

otosan

I

I see him standing
over thirty years ago
on the train platform
hair pitch black
years from today's silver
his uniform blue
hat gripping his head leaving a crease
takes him hours to comb out
white gloves wrap firmly around the lantern swinging by his side
chest pushed out proudly
always a smile
his teeth only now beginning to overlap & darken

he looks along glistening tracks
above the crowd of waiting passengers
pulls his hat down low
just over his eyes
like the soldiers he saw as a boy
the golden "J" and "R" of his hat just catch the light
he checks the train schedule & for a moment
chinese history of the *kanji* he studied spins through his head
ancient poems ringing in his memory

a young woman passes in *kimono*
he smiles
the sound of her *geta* against the pavement
the flower pattern across her back
perfume hanging in the air
it holds him there
he thinks of his wife pregnant
with his second daughter

"oh, if I has a son. I don't have no son"
his self-taught English
tripping across the dim light of this kitchen table
over thirty years later
after three daughters born & married
after the birth of grandsons
his wife giggling, pouring tea
right hand covering her mouth

"yes, but you have grandsons"
my voice young and hopeful
he looks down
left hand rubbing his tea cup
"yes, um . . . *nandake, nandake . . .*"
head comes up
eyes closing slowly behind rimless glasses
eyelids fluttering like wings of cicadas
he's lost in one million alphabets
fishing for the right words
mouth struggling around foreign syllables
"grandsons, not my same name . . . my same name is dead with me"
silence
a light steam rises from our tea cups
like mount fuji mist
just before dawn

II

I have never asked you what happened that day
did you see it coming
hear it
feel the rumbling underfoot
did you step out into the air like a leaf
a puff of smoke
did it sneak up from behind like a friend

your hands held in front of you, a shield
white gloves, flakes of snow falling
slow motion
did you spin
reaching for the platform
arms pedalling
I have never asked you what flashed before your eyes
what you heard
if you felt the impact
saw the eyes of the driver
the blood
I have never asked you

III

I first met you at yokohama city hall
sweating from my tokyo bus ride
tie gripping at my neck
I saw you enter smoothly
straw hat, bermuda shirt
a gift from thailand
one of your previous boarders
you walked around the large table
as if you'd built it yourself
the oldest man in the room
you stood in front of me and smiled
tried to pronounce my name
I almost went to shake your hand
bowed instead
noticing the plastic

we walked to the taxi
you struggling with my carry-on
the limp very subtle
right foot touching down

just before it should
the taxi ride filled with empty sounds
my body still on canadian time
the driver telling me things about this city
you beside me, back straight, hand in your lap
fiddling with the straw of your hat

we stopped at your house
I dragged my suitcase up your steps
shirt sticking to my back from the July heat
you opened the door
your wife stood in her apron
hands joined lightly in front of her
bowing
I stepped inside

IV

your body is lying in the hospital bed
not yet 30
barely alive
your family standing over you
wife ripe
about to give birth
parents worried silent
like a funeral
your heart beating slowly
drowning in your chest
eyes closed
no longer there

you are a boy again
before the war
before the train
youngest child of 13
running along the streets of your seaside hometown
laughing with friends the sun touching down
licking at your bare shoulders

"he will live"
the doctor's voice motionless
"his heart is strong
did he play an instrument?"

you smile crookedly telling me how your wife watched as
you played the *yokobuye* flute at the town festival
she grins passing me another bowl of rice
"he was very good"

V

now I sometimes visit you
a pilgrimage into your mind
japanese characters written left-handed
on scraps of paper
the smell of your home stays with me
this poem un
finished
writes itself in my mind
with every step
along the river bank
the sound of my breath

the river

under the moon

his hair. black. sprinkled with strands of silver-grey. even eyebrows
streaked subtly. face wide & pulled tight relaxing only under
his eyes. I can see his paintings. the ones he gave me on picture
postcards. the ones he showed me piled up on shelves in the
junior high school's art room. the ones in oil a flurry of colour
dancing across the canvas. wings of butterflies hidden in every
shadow. he painted these ten years ago. you can melt into them
if you're not careful. now he does only *kirie*. traditional japanese
paper cutting. a pattern cut delicately into a black sheet of paper
revealing the white. he tells me balance is very important. cuts
sometimes through 2 or 3 layers making copies for friends "I like
it very much, with *kirie* you have no chance for mistakes"

his hands are thick. rough like the men I have seen in the fields
near my apartment. hands hard from ploughing the earth,
beating stalks, every so often popping their heads up to check on
their wives. I step into his school studio. young female students
giggling in corners at the size of my nose. I tell him how I love
art & he sits me down a brother, a son. outside it's raining like
vancouver. like the one night I spent in london.

he explains the family of primary colours in japanese & shows
me students' artwork. scenes of temples, samurai demons & gods.
picture him hours back bent, hands moving the knife a spider.
he turns to me across the table scattered with art books. the girls
watching from across the room. "*gekka bijin* flower, you know?"
looks at me plainly. eyes unmoving waiting. his chin tilted slightly
inward, a young boy. he's almost fifty. begins flipping through
pages stopping at the picture of a small white flower in bloom &
writes the *kanji* characters for its name. "this means moon. this
means under. this means beautiful. this means person. beautiful
person under moon. *gekka bijin*, beautiful woman, like venus you
know?"

only 5 or 6 times a year around midnight the flower opens. he
tells me he has some at his house & then silence. the after-meal
silence when the only sound that fills the room is the pouring of
green tea. the steam crawling. "please come to my house tonight
to see the *gekka bijin*. but I tell him I can't. a month later I arrive
at school & on my desk is an enlarged photograph of the night
of the flower opening. petals pure white so delicate they look like
powder & I can see the wings of butterflies.

we are now standing at the window watching as the rain falls
silent slow motion. students making their way home rows of
umbrellas covering blue uniforms like turtle shells. skirts barely
reach the girls' knees slowly making their way to high school
miniskirt length. "I will tell you a secret" his voice a whisper. hand
cupping the side of his face. "I have *katana*, sword, you know?"
he puts his hands together a samurai sword & slashes the air in
one smooth stroke. "after the world war the second americans
come here to japan & take all *katana*. but my father keep. he
dug & put in the earth very deep." hands move in front of us like
the blades of two shovels. "under a big tree he put two *katana*
in special oil paper no water can touch. it was under the big tree
for 40 years then he remembered & dig again. one *katana* not so
good but one o.k. only small broken." picks up a pencil draws
the blade with little nicks in it "I fixed. I know how to make it
sharp now it's o.k. I have licence, you know? but it is a secret." the
hand cupping his mouth again. six months later his wife has lung
cancer. they remove part of both her lungs.

I leave the room bowing. walking in the rain want to peel my
shirt off like old skin & run like a boy. feet carrying me past
pachinko parlours & noodle shops. soon the sun will set. walk
down the hill leading to my small apartment. only the sound of
falling rain in the dead end of my street. footsteps echoing up
the narrow staircase. neighbours' doors locked. I imagine them
crouched against the peephole watching my every move. it's night
& I lie here on my futon. rain against the window. outside the
moon almost full.

morning

out my apartment
down the narrow staircase
dead-end street
turn the corner

fuji majestic horizon
white sun rising
chiselled into sky
as if to say
you are nothing but this breath
the moon full pale & fading
rides high

fuji – the moon – in blue morning sky
caught like lovers sharing a cigarette
the sound of the river framing them

fuji

night
      two hours from the top
I can see
almost touch it
head spinning on some unknown axis

behind me
shadows & silhouettes
down)
      shoulder-to-shoulder
lanterns hanging in the air
      connecting us
as though we're holding hands
holding the world
up)
      the tops of our heads
the pain shooting from my calves
drowning
no one smiles
just the push & shove)
      trying to reach the top for sunrise
fingers numb
toes frozen together with fear
waiting to go home

sky brightens
we're at a stand still
silence)
      every so often a woman drops to her knees
& vomits on the side of the trail
down)
      her husband rubs her back
looking over his shoulder embarrassed

sun breaks in
we take a breath at the sight of a sea of clouds
white)
        rolling cross the horizon
horses frozen mid-stride
lanterns flick off
shoulders relax
body)
        language loose after seven hours
drunk laughing through crisp air

kinkakuji, the temple of the golden pavilion

kyoto. *kinkakuji.* three-levelled temple. covered in gold. kyoko-chi pond. a mirror of glass. golden echo. stone islands. tree trimmed beauty. I'm here with my friend john. we're english teachers from yokohama. it's 1 p.m. we've had only 2 hours sleep. still drunk from drinking all night. this is not about a canadian and an englishman teaching in japan. this is not about the *gaijin* experience. this temple glowing gold. magnificent. upstages even the sun. was built in 1397. for shogun *yoshimitsu.* burnt down in 1950. rebuilt in 1955. this is not about history. then there's mishima yukio's story of the young obsessed zen monk who set the temple on fire. but this is not about japanese literature or the contrast between old and new. about japanese temples beside vending machines. this is not about . . .

we're standing at the edge of *kyoko-chi* pond. heads numb. brains shrunk from lack of water. from five days of drinking. from only 15 hours sleep. john's hands are shaking & I'm sweating as if we were standing in the middle of africa. "*shashin! shashin!* please, take picture. *shashin!* picture, please." school girls giggling spastically. salarymen tie-less in golf shirts smoke cigarettes like breathing. there are a couple of tokyo hookers beside us. tight pants. high heels & sunglasses. dyed hair. lipstick. one is wearing a black t-shirt. the white writing reads, "natural beauty". let's pose in front of the golden pavilion. shimmering lake. like a postcard. "*shashin! shashin! shashin!*"

you know there's something to be said about being hung-over in front of a national treasure. john says, "fantastic!" the gold a magnet. a mirror. a mecca. a mantra. a medal. a maze. for a moment you're mesmerized as sobering eyes lick every corner. doorway. window frame. until you hear the cry of the phoenix golden mounted in the center of the roof. its feet frozen. welded together. oh, how it looks like it wants to fly. break free. *kinkakuji.* fantastic!

in the gift shop you can buy t-shirts & postcards. golden
miniatures. books on zen. scrolls. sweet or salty crackers & cakes.
or sit in the roadside open air restaurant on tatami mats covered
in red cloth & slurp your noodles loudly. sip on some sake while
taking in the delicate beauty. we walked past & through stopping
momentarily at a photograph of *kinkakuji* in mid-winter. snow
sprinkling surrounding trees. temple reflected crisply in the lake.
the phoenix naked. we walked slowly. noticing the trees. stones.
the women. yet nothing is as gold. golden. gold.

on our way out. we are stopped by students. "excuse me. may I
speak english to you. my name is yuka. is this first time kyoto? do
you like *kinkakuji*? can I picture with me?" she smiles. her friends
giggle. everything is golden & nothing can faze us. not even their
pedophile-looking guide who is touching them far too much.
not even the stares we get. whispered comments at our height.
the size of our noses. our feet. the look of surprise when we use
chopsticks. not even the repeated questions of whether we are able
to eat raw fish or rice can faze us now.

but wait. what I really wanted to say was that for one moment I
was lost. melted. the gold. the phoenix. as if I had stepped into
a postcard. I really wanted to say that I was hung over. delirious.
caught by the light. the gold. the reflection. really I wanted to say
that it must have been a trick of the sun. an illusion. the gold. a
careful placing of mirrors. the balance of paint. but what I really
wanted to say would have taken far less paper. less ink. less time.

yokohama dentures

I saw him in the basement cafeteria of the yokohama city hall
building. he was in a dark business suit, tie. the standard uniform
in his sixties or early fifties even. the sound of men slurping
their noodles and sipping tea, a waterfall of sounds. he sat, just
finished a bowl of soba himself. had that calm sober look that
early digestion often brings. black- rimmed glasses balanced on
the bridge of his nose like a diamond cutter. with a sweep of his
hand he held his dentures delicately in a pair of chopsticks. kept
them just hovering over his bowl centimetres in front of his face.
every so often he would pick at them with a toothpick then dip
them into a cup of water. there was a certain gracefulness about
the whole thing. a certain flick of the wrist, posture of his back.
the deep slow breathing as if it were an ancient art form. the
ikebana of denture cleaning. finished he popped them back into
his mouth, gulped his tea and stood to leave without a single drop
on his suit.

karma police
after Radiohead

the karma police are going to catch up with me sooner or later. I've slipped off the eight fold path. I woke up full of regret. for the time I never smiled and the whole day went bad. I'm reborn as a cow, as a speck of sand on a war torn beach. this is what you get, I guess, when you talk in maths in fractions. when your heart is tangled up in algorithms. my *samsara* wheel's spun badly. I never meant to have hitler hair. I'm sorry for making you feel ill. I know now that all it takes is to breathe. to have pure thoughts, smile and salute the sun. I lost myself for a minute there. I'm born again in the eye of the storm. they're after me. the sound of siddhartha's sirens fill the room. this is what you get. I can feel the karmic cuffs, the furrowed brow. I've given all I can but it's not enough.

hong kong, china

sound of this downtown tram
slicing the street of herbal remedy shops
filipino women near central station on sundays
exchanging letters from manilan lovers

I meet his eyes in the window
snake skins hang in spiralling coils
fins of shark and turtle shells
he knows me
sees through me
man in the back grinding something
woman smiles in the corner
arms crossed

dried fish floating vapours
balloning ovals of bone-filled jars
a peek into the grinding bowl heals blindness
rub of my elbow into ground-up sea horse
makes my hair grow
while slivers of deer antler in my tea
will give me a hard-on for a week

what are you grinding? I ask
tiger claw, antelope tail bone,
a monkey's floating rib, peacock feet?
tea
he answers smiling

the whole day changes colour

nha trang, vietnam

there's the pamphlet that we picked up in the war museum. the one with the black & white photograph of smiling american soldiers crouched down on a jungled beach. they've set up a row of vietcong heads in front of them, trophies.

this beach in january. the way the wind picks up the water in waves. in distant hills, from some hollywood movie, the sound of helicopters.

cyclo rickshaw drivers call to us like fruit vendors, "you want boom, boom? young girl? you smoke maruwana?" for a dollar you get pedaled halfway across the city, told the life story of 6 children, a wife, mother-in-law, no food, no money & a string of relatives who live in your home country. all for a dollar, "you want boom, boom? young girl? you smoke maruwana?"

last week in the streets of hanoi, we got lost in front of water puppet theatres, rows of shoe stores dreamed of fried egg rolls & now here, on this beach the day is full up with history.

for a moment the clouds turn orange. at every corner postcard kids shoeless & round-eyed like stray dogs meet us. there was the girl in hue, in a yellow sun hat in front of the post office & the boy in the cafe who we gave money to buy shoes.

here on this beach, after midnight, transvestite hookers give blowjobs. you can buy red t-shirts with yellow stars or rent young smooth skinned boys.

everywhere, women with triangle hats made of straw. pyramids moving in markets of raw meat hanging on hooks, turtles weighed for soup. a young girl with a big smile shows us vietnam silk. school girls in white *ao dias* silk dresses ride by on bicycles like angels, folds of white tucked under their arms. we sit at a corner café, cameras poised, while a legless man offers to shine our shoes.

on this beach there's the boy with no limbs who hobbles on stumps to the edge of our chair. the old man who smells of aftershave, his white *ho chi minh* beard, black teeth, open christ hands cast shadows over our tan. we ignore him. he goes away & comes back as a woman carrying her skin & bones son with glass eyes. a boy with no arms. a blind man with half a head of hair selling g.i. lighters or a young girl who offers us sex.

here, on this beach, the sun explodes softly.

4

I'm astounded by people who want to 'know' the universe when it's
hard enough to find your way around Chinatown.

–Woody Allen

a clever title that hints at the poem's theme

this is the point in the poem
where I slip in a simile
like a flick of a magician's wrist
out flies a dove
or your missing card

the point where the images
come through clearly
hit all your senses
the fresh field
the dewy wet green grass
light breeze
the way the sun lounges
yawning through the dawn

where I make you feel
as though I know you
as though I am talking about
what you went through last night
you think
how does he know me?
how did he capture
in words my pain
the way I feel?

this is where
I cut the poem short
leave you with a final thought
something that forces you
to push your lips together
in a soft hum
as though you took a sip of rich coffee
as though you just slipped
into a tub of warm water

aaron

you can't help but think
that there was a moment before
the real fame
before the cadillacs
the suede shoes
the movies
hawaii

maybe just after his first hit single
on the way to the record studio
just before his name
becomes household

when he still feels like
he can step out of the car for burgers
the young lady at the counter
recognizes his voice

are you?

sorry miss
the name's aaron

she hands him the food shaking
he's cool but still shy enough to smile
takes the paper bag from her
remembers his southern manners
turns

thank you
his lip twitches
thank you very much

audrey

there was a way she entered rooms. the trickle of a smile as she
glided across the floor. like a slow-moving spring breeze. as a
child in nazi-occupied holland she learned to hold her breath
while passing german soldiers. learned to look innocent as though
already in front of the camera.

the light in her eyes endured the murder of relatives. starvation.
she survived by eating tulip bulbs.

she learned to walk. between the rays of the sun as she carried
secret messages for the resistance in her ballet shoes.

up spanish steps in rome at tiffany's for breakfast with her funny
face in paris she never forgets.

van

walks into a french field
points his gun to his chest
and fires
just missing his heart
he walks home dizzy
crawls into bed
and bleeds
lights a pipe
his brother theo visits
the doctor says
they can't get the bullet out
he dies
sun flowers spinning
melting into nights
full of stars

wrong
when the walls bend, with your breathing
– Radiohead

there's something wrong
there's the flat sound of air
settling in the corners
the shifting in plastic chairs
no one wants to move too much
for fear of being noticed

last chance
last call
there's something wrong
when they feel the need
to smoke up at 9:30 a.m.
I can only do so much
when the student is ready
the teacher will appear
so here I am

her eyes ask
sir, can you help me?
I'm pregnant again
I haven't slept all night
I took some bad drugs
I can't do it
I'm stupid

the room spins
late again he sits down
body language
the angle of his spine
please don't hit me
please don't rat me out
to the police
one more toke
& everything will be all right

the world is burning up
at the edges
the day spilling at the seams
sir, could you teach me?
save me
fuck you, sir

if there was one word
one zen slap
to turn on a light
I'd say it
but your world is all about
the hookups
the back door connections
the counterfeit 50 dollar bills

fuck it
we don't need to try
nothing's free
the right clothes
right music
do what the t.v. says
I need another toke
a blow job
isn't really having sex
sir, can you help me?
generation x-y-z
we're running out of letters
running out of explanations
the walls are bending

you

the sound of your heart beating fills this room. the doctor presses
against your mother's smooth belly which is just preparing for the
expansion of you. the *pa-ra-pa-pa-pum* of your drumming heart.
a high speed fetal coded message. my heart stops, eyes locked
with your mother's. this moment you are for real. this thumb-
tap of your heart. the dripping of a leaking middle-of-the-night
faucet brings the reality of this miracle about to happen home.
I imagine the shape of your face. the smell of you just woken
from an afternoon nap. I breathe you in close to me. the touch of
your skin soft against my neck. your eyes will hold the secrets of
centuries. I'll pour into you all the moments I hold dear through
the dilations of my pupils like intermittent waterfalls. will your
feet look like mine? the shape of your ears? will my mother catch
the edge of your silhouette in the bath and think you are me
as she flashes back three decades? your own mother, her smile,
in between the echoing beats of your heart, splashes all over
this room. in months I will kneel in front of her in our kitchen
and speak softly to you through her belly between moist kisses.
she will know that our love grows larger through every beating
movement.

cole's notes

1.
your mother punches through
the waves of labour on this couch
breathing your arrival
the way she focuses
on the sound of the air in the room
as if she could see between
your heartbeats
my hands warm on her shoulders
if I could lift her with wings
carry her above all of this
we call the doctor
it might take another 15 hours
one more hour
her body becomes a fist
we leave speeding
your mother says,
it feels like we're moving so fast
I'm glad you waited for the wee hours
the triage nurse is not impressed
no water breaking?
she moves barely lifting her feet
looks at your mother as if
she was faking the pain behind deep moans
the room changes tempo
from piano to allegro
as they discover
your mother's 6 centimetres dilated
20 minutes go by like an exhalation
one walk down the hall
she is at 8
we move to the labour room

2.
with every push your heartbeat drops
like god having fun with the pause button
my empty stomach makes my head spin dizzy
I sit down against the wall
the room is an outer body experience
you slip out blue and frowning
like an angry fish you grunt instead of cry
they rush you to intensive care for observation
I stay with you
little electrodes taped to your wee chest
you grip my thumb like a ladder rung

3.
your jet black elvis hair and sideburns
make the nurses swoon
little twitch of your upper lip is so flirtatious
little do they know it's just gas
the cleaning woman comes to mop your room
complaining of a bad knee
until she sees you and melts

4.

        cole porter
        coleslaw
   roller colester
  nat king cole
        coleman stove
        cole miner's daughter
 coca cole-a
  old king cole
st. nicoleas
holly cole
        coleiseum
        coleogne
        coleossus
christopher coleumbus
 coled-cuts
 cole

v.

I am not afraid of your fragility. the thin liquid twigs of your
fingers. tiny little ice cream feet. your six-pound frame. I have
seen people lift you like a rare chinese vase made of leaf-thin
crystal. I hold you like an extra limb. the whisper of your breath
against my upper arm. your eyes open I lay you out over my
thigh. tell you stories of when I met your mother. your eyes,
focusing mere inches in front of your face.

variations

You must read this while listening to Bach: The Goldberg Variations of 1742, an "Aria with 30 variations". Listen to it on a pre-seven a.m. morning, the sun just barely awake, its bed head rays of light slipping through windows. Listen to the Glenn Gould 1955 recording--the one done in an abandoned Presbyterian Chapel at 207 Thirtieth Street. If you can, try reading this in June: a hot New York sort of June with the sounds of summer muffling though the walls. What is most essential for this reading are your clothes. Go to your winter closet and get a Harris Tweed jacket and sweater, a long winter overcoat, a Shetland wool scarf, a cap pulled down low and a pair of gloves. Find a comfy seat near the stereo or better yet a piano where you can feel the music's vibrations. Close your eyes and imagine this man: shaggy hair, dark eyes, torso rocking like a metronome, skinny fingers moving virtuoso over ivory. Make your hands into tight fists, letting them open slowly imagine how it feels to know that before playing, Gould would plunge his hands and lower arms, like some Shaolin Kung fu monk, into boiling hot water.

the early light plays piano tricks
over the wooden floor
gould's hands boil up the stereo
"the marlon brando of the piano"
cole
mid-room
stops crawling to pick up a spoon
smiling up at me he bangs the floor
variation thirty
one

somewhere we have never traveled
after e.e. cummings

here today is tomorrow
rest of our lives
opening up like a flower

forever is a place
we have never been
here we are at the boarding call
you & I
suddenly I'm afraid to fly

your smile calms me
your hand
& eyes hold more secrets than
the scent of rare roses

let us travel then
through the lines in our palms
like rivers
making souvenirs of slow kisses
there are no footprints here to follow
only the slow flutter of our hearts